The Bill of Rights in Today's World

by Ted Henson

illustrated by Milton Hall

cover by Jeff Van Kanegan

photo credit © Corel Weststock

Publisher
Instructional Fair • TS Denison
Grand Rapids, Michigan 49544

Instructional Fair • TS Denison grants the individual purchaser permission to reproduce patterns and student activity materials in this book for noncommercial individual or classroom use only. Reproduction for an entire school or school system is strictly prohibited. No other part of this publication may be reproduced in whole or in part. No part of this publication may be reproduced for storage in a retrieval system, or transmitted in any form or by any means, electronic, mechanical, recording, or otherwise, without the prior written permission of the publisher. For information regarding permission, write to Instructional Fair • TS Denison, P.O. Box 1650, Grand Rapids, MI 49501.

ISBN: 1-56822-919-4
The Bill of Rights in Today's World
Copyright © 2000 by Instructional Fair Group
a Tribune Education Company
3195 Wilson Drive NW
Grand Rapids, Michigan 49544

All Rights Reserved • Printed in the USA

Table of Contents

Why Was the Bill of Rights Added? 1
Meet James Madison 3
The First Amendment Rights 5
Freedom of Religion 6
Freedom of Expression 8
Freedom of the Press 10
The Right of Assembly and Petition 12
The Second Amendment—The Right of the People to Keep and Bear Arms 14
The Second Amendment Today 16
The Third Amendment—The Quartering of Troops 17
The Third Amendment Today 19
The Fourth Amendment—Freedom from Unreasonable Searches and Seizures 21
The Fourth Amendment Today 23
The Fifth Amendment—Rights in Criminal Cases 25
The Grand Jury and Due Process of Law 27
The Miranda Rights 29
The Sixth Amendment—The Right to a Fair Trial 30
The Right to a Public Trial 32
The Seventh Amendment—Civil Court Trials 33
The Seventh Amendment Today 35
The Eighth Amendment 36
Cruel and Unusual Punishment 37
The Ninth Amendment—Other Rights of the People 39
The Tenth Amendment—Powers to the State 41
Answer Key 43

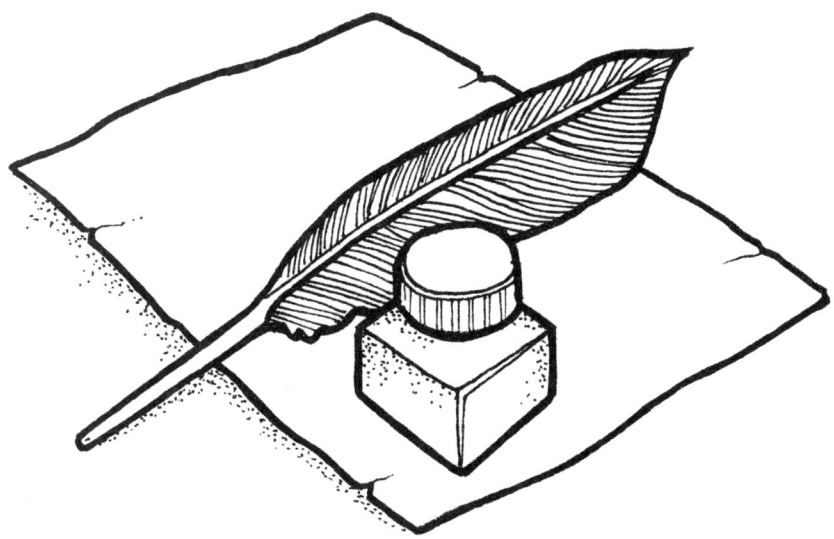

Introduction

In the summer of 1787 representatives from the 13 states met in Philadelphia to draw up a plan of government for the United States of America. The result of that meeting was the Constitution of the United States. This plan set up a system of self-government unlike that of any other nation.

However, many people felt that something was missing from this document. It did not provide for citizens a list of individual rights that were protected by law. As a result, the constitution was amended in 1791. Ten amendments were added to help protect individual liberties. These ten amendments are now called the *Bill of Rights*.

The purpose of this book is to present students with information on the Bill of Rights, the first ten amendments to the Constitution of the United States. The instructional activities have been carefully selected and organized to provide students with useful information as well as practice in developing needed skills. Each informational page provides a brief story about the Bill of Rights. Following these stories, review questions are provided as a checkup on what students have read. Finally, questions are given that will require students to use high-order thinking skills to successfully complete the activity.

These lessons are designed for teachers who want students to be actively involved in their own learning. The material is not organized to conform to any conventional textbook; instead, it is organized to suit the purpose of the teacher who wants to either supplement or complement the text. Each page begins with a story followed by review questions and finally a question for discussion. Thus students are engaged in both direct recall and application.

The informational pages can either be read to students or duplicated for them to read by themselves or in small groups. Some of the exercises can be done verbally by the teacher as a direct whole-class discussion, as small collaborative group activities, or completed as independent activities.

The purpose of this approach is to present implementation of instruction based on research-grounded procedures. The activities should 1) enhance recall of factual information, 2) improve comprehension of textual material, 3) provide opportunity for inquiry, and 4) involve students in both experiential and collaborative learning. By using a variety of approaches in the classroom, students begin to realize the tie between the current activity and learning how to learn. The work then becomes more meaningful and helps students become more responsible for their own learning.

Name _____

Why Was the Bill of Rights Added?

When the Constitutional Convention met on May 25, 1787, in the Pennsylvania State House, it was attempting to do what had never been done before. These men were setting up a new government with limited powers that were being granted to it by the people. Up to this time all attempts to limit government had been made after the government was already in place and the attempts were to reduce its power. Thus the Constitution of the United States was to become a unique document in the world.

The Constitutional Convention worked through the summer of 1787, and the new document was ready for final consideration on September 12, 1787. On September 15, 1787, Edmund Randolph of Virginia proposed that amendments be made by the state conventions and then turned over to another general convention for consideration. However, his arguments were in vain, as the convention voted unanimously in favor of the Constitution. The convention adjourned on September 17, 1787. The next step was ratification by the 13 states.

The call for amendments began to spread across the country. James Madison, who was now being called the Father of the Constitution, was opposed to such a list, as were most of the leaders of the Federalists. The Federalists were those people who supported the ratification of the Constitution. Madison believed that, since the Constitution was written to give limited powers to the new government, a list of individual rights was not necessary. Alexander Hamilton of New York joined him in this belief. Together they wrote a series of essays, now called *The Federalist Papers*, which supported ratification of the new Constitution. These papers were widely printed throughout the sates. The Anti-Federalists worked to defeat the Constitution.

When it became apparent that the Constitution was in trouble and might not be ratified, Madison and other Federalists began to rethink the issue of a list of individual rights. On June 21, 1789, New Hampshire became the ninth state to ratify the Constitution, meaning that it had won the approval of the states. Madison and Hamilton now worked harder and were successful in winning ratification in both Virginia and New York. However, the people were still calling for the list of rights.

Madison became convinced that a bill of rights was necessary to ensure acceptance of the Constitution. As one of the representatives from Virginia to the First Federal Congress, he was able to get through 17 amendments in the early months of the Congress. This number was later reduced to 12 in the Senate. On October 2, 1789, President Washington sent each state a copy of the 12 amendments adopted by Congress. By December 5, 1791, three fourths of the states had ratified the 10 amendments that became the Bill of Rights.

Name _____

I. Reviewing the Facts

1. When and where did the Constitutional Convention meet? _____
   _____

2. Who was called the Father of the Constitution? _____

3. Madison and _____ wrote a series of essays supporting the Constitution that are known today as the _____.

4. Two political groups were formed during the debate over the Constitution. One supported the Constitution and the other opposed it. What were the names of these political groups?
   _____ and _____

5. _____ became the ninth state to ratify (meaning that it had won the approval of the states) the Constitution.

6. Madison was able to get through _____ amendments in the Congress, but this number was reduced to _____ in the Senate. The number approved by the states was _____.

7. _____, the first president, sent 12 amendments to the states for approval.

8. By _____, three fourths of the states had ratified what is now known as the Bill of Rights.

II. Thinking About the Story

1. The Constitution of the United States that was written in 1787 in Philadelphia became an important document for many reasons. It set up a new government and accomplished something never done in government before. Explain below why this is such an important document and what the delegates were able to accomplish for the first time in history.

   _____
   _____
   _____
   _____
   _____

2. The debate over the Constitution quickly turned into a debate over whether or not a list of individual rights should be added. Take the side of either the Federalists or the Anti-Federalists and make an argument either for or against the addition of a Bill of Rights. Write your arguments below.

   _____
   _____
   _____
   _____

Name _____

Meet James Madison

James Madison was born on March 16, 1751, in Port Conway, Virginia. He was raised on the Madison Plantation, Montpelier, near Orange, Virginia. Madison was a frail and sickly child. He studied at the Donald Robertson School in King and Queen County, Virginia. He later attended the College of New Jersey (now Princeton University). He studied very hard and graduated in two years in 1771. Madison had a deep interest in religion, so he spent six months studying Hebrew and philosophy. However, his weak speaking voice kept him from becoming a minister. He then became interested in law and was well read in that area.

In 1777 Madison helped to draft a new Virginia Constitution and the Virginia Declaration of Rights. These documents would serve as models for several other states. He served in the Continental Congress from 1780 until 1783, when he returned to Virginia. He had planned to study law, but these studies were interrupted when he was elected to the Virginia Assembly for three successive one-year terms. In the assembly Madison continued Thomas Jefferson's fight for separation of church and state. There was a movement to provide state support for teachers of the Christian religion. However, in 1786 the state assembly passed Virginia's Statute of Religious Freedom.

In 1787 Madison was elected to the Constitutional Convention in Philadelphia. In spite of his young age (36 years old), he took a major role in the convention. He worked hard to provide a stronger central government. He also kept a complete record of the proceedings at the convention. These records provide much of what we know today about the convention. In fact, Madison played such a key role at the convention that he was given the nickname Father of the Constitution. He also played a major role in the process of ratifying the Constitution.

Though he originally opposed the idea of adding a list of individual rights to the Constitution, he later changed his mind and became a supporter of such a list. He saw that refusing to make such an addition to the Constitution could result in losing widespread support for the document. He also came to see that such amendments might indeed be beneficial for the new nation.

When he became a member of the new Federal Congress, he was able to push through what is now known as the Bill of Rights. While in Congress, Madison supported the policies of George Washington until Alexander Hamilton, Washington's secretary of the treasury, outlined his plan for the financial program. Madison felt that the plan favored wealthy Easterners at the expense of the ordinary citizen. As a result he turned against the Washington administration and Hamilton's Federalist Party. He and Thomas Jefferson would join together in 1792 to form the Democratic-Republican Party, the forerunner of the present-day Democratic Party.

Madison later served as secretary of state during the Jefferson presidency. In 1808 Madison was elected president of the United States. Trade disputes with France and England were the most serious problems facing the new president. In 1810 Congress passed a law reopening trade with both countries. However, if one of the countries would agree to stop interfering with American commerce, trade would be stopped with the other country. France announced that it would revoke the blockade against American trade with Great Britain, so Madison stopped all trade with

Britain. However, Napoleon refused to honor his agreement. Americans were angered at Napoleon and at Britain, which continued to stop American ships and force some sailors to join the British Navy.

Finally, on July 1, 1812, Madison asked Congress to declare war on Great Britain. The War of 1812 lasted until the Treaty of Ghent was signed in 1815. There was no clear winner of the war. The Americans had stopped the British invasion of the country on two fronts, but the British had prevented the Americans from taking Canada and had burned Washington, D.C. However, American territorial claims had been preserved.

After the war, the Federalist Party declined in national importance because of its opposition to the war. National trade began to expand, and the country experienced great economic growth. In 1816 Madison created the country's second national bank. He also approved the Tariff of 1816, which introduced the principle of protecting American industries.

After his term in office, Madison returned to Virginia and Montpelier. In 1826 he followed Jefferson as president of the University of Virginia. He died at Montpelier on June 28, 1836.

I. Thinking About the Story
1. James Madison is noted for many things in his life, including being called the Father of the United States Constitution. What do you consider the most important contribution made by Madison during his life? Explain your answer below.

_____
_____
_____
_____
_____
_____

2. At first, James Madison opposed the addition of a list of individual rights. However, later he changed his mind and was responsible for pushing through such a list. Why do you think he changed his mind? What does this tell you about the kind of leader that James Madison was becoming?

_____
_____
_____
_____
_____
_____

The First Amendment Rights

Congress shall make no law respecting an establishment of religion, or prohibiting the free exercise thereof, or abridging the freedom of speech or of the press; or the right of the people peaceably to assemble, and to petition the Government for a redress of grievances.

The First Amendment to the Constitution is cited so frequently that many people believe that the rights guaranteed were part of the original Constitution. Five fundamental liberties are guaranteed the citizens of the United States in this one amendment. Those liberties include religion, speech, press, assembly, and petition.

Many of the early settlers came to the New World because they were trying to escape religious persecution in Europe. However, they were disappointed as laws developed in some of the colonies establishing official churches and limiting the rights of citizens who failed to belong to a preferred religion. Lack of freedom of speech and expression was another major reason that people left Europe. It also played a large role in the grievances listed against the British government when independence was declared. Freedom of the press goes along very closely with the freedom of speech. From the trial of John Peter Zenger to the fight for independence, there was strong support for citizens to have the right to publish their ideas and opinions without censorship from the government. The final two freedoms go hand in hand. The lack of freedom of assembly and the ability to petition the government for grievances were major reasons for the movement of settlers to America. Unfortunately, they found the same problems here under British rule that they had experienced back home in Europe.

After the American Revolution, there was a desire among the citizens to safeguard all of these freedoms by adding them to the Constitution. These freedoms are such a large part of our everyday lives that we will consider each freedom individually in this book.

Thinking About the First Amendment Rights

Try to imagine your life without the five freedoms listed in the First Amendment. Write below ways that your life would be changed if these freedoms had not been guaranteed in the Bill of Rights and were no longer in effect in the United States.

_____
_____
_____
_____
_____
_____

Freedom of Religion

The First Amendment of the Bill of Rights provides a person the right to practice whatever faith he or she chooses or the right to have no religious beliefs at all. From the beginning of this country, the desire for religious freedom was one of the major reasons for the settlement of America. Puritans and other religious groups came to the New World to escape persecution in Europe.

However, the concept of religious freedom was not firmly established in this country until the American Revolution. Thomas Jefferson and James Madison were successful in getting Virginia to adopt a Statute of Religious Liberty in 1786. This law prohibited a state church in Virginia and guaranteed the right for citizens in Virginia to practice religion as they wished. This established the climate that encouraged James Madison to write a similar law into the Bill of Rights.

The First Amendment originally only protected religious groups from unfair treatment by the federal government. However, this protection did not prove to be sufficient. Several states including Connecticut and Massachusetts set up official churches. This meant that the state government supported those churches. In addition, the state of New Hampshire prohibited nonProtestants from holding office until the mid 1800s. Finally in the 1940s the Supreme Court upheld that the states must ensure First Amendment guarantees of religious freedom. This put an official end to any state-sponsored church in the United States.

The First Amendment guarantees the freedom of religion through two clauses in the Bill of Rights. The first is known as the *establishment clause*. This clause says that the government cannot establish an official religion in this country or show preference to one religion over another. This is the clause that is generally referred to when people speak of the separation of church and state.

The second clause is the *free exercise* clause that means that the government cannot, in most cases, interfere with the way a person practices religion. However, this does not mean that the government must allow all religious practices. For example, in the 1800s some members of the Mormon religion believed that a man had a religious duty to have more than one wife. In 1878 the Supreme Court upheld a federal law against polygamy, which means having more than one wife. The courts agreed with the view of most Americans that polygamy was harmful to society.

Most people agree that the original intent of the First Amendment was to prohibit the establishment of an official religion in this country and to prohibit the government from showing preference to one religion. However, this issue has taken on new meaning in its interpretation today. In various court cases, government activity related to religion has been upheld in some instances and struck down in other cases. For example, the courts have ruled that bus transportation may be used to carry parochial school students and that the "blue laws" may be enforced. Blue laws require businesses in some towns to remain closed during church hours. At the same time a government plan to provide financial aid to religious schools was prohibited by the courts.

Name _____

The issue of freedom of religion continues to be argued today. Issues such as school prayer and public school curricula continue to be debated. On one side are those who think that religious fundamentalists and organizations such as the Christian Coalition are trying to impose their beliefs on society and undermine the secular tradition of institutions such as the public schools. On the other side are those who complain that this society allows insufficient attention, and accords no priority, to religious beliefs, especially in instruction and textbooks used in the public schools. This situation is being made even more complicated by the changing religious composition of the United States. In addition to Christians and Jews, there are growing numbers of Muslims, Hindus, Buddhists, and other believers, as well as nonbelievers in our society. The arguments that started before the American Revolution are likely to continue for a long time in the future.

I. Reviewing the Facts
1. What are the two main clauses that provide for freedom of religion in the First Amendment? _____
_____

2. What law passed in Virginia in 1789 helped to set the stage for religious freedom in the United States? _____
3. How did the Supreme Court decision in the 1940s help ensure freedom of religion for all citizens of the United States? _____
_____

4. In 1878 the Supreme Court upheld the decision that some members of the Mormon religion must stop practicing _____, which meant that men had more than one wife.
5. Give an example of a government activity relating to religion that has been approved by the courts and one that has been overturned. Approved: _____
_____
_____

Overturned: _____
_____
_____

II. Thinking About the Story
1. The religious composition of American society is changing rapidly. Many more religious groups are growing in numbers. How do you think this change in society will affect the debate over issues dealing with religion in society?
_____
_____
_____
_____

2. Conduct a debate in your classroom on the following issue: the government should or should not provide direct financial assistance to students attending church-supported schools.

Freedom of Expression

When the First Amendment speaks of the freedom of expression, it really is talking about the freedom of speech. This is another of the cornerstones of American democracy. It is one of the reasons that many early settlers left Europe to come to the New World. It was also one of the goals of the American colonists which led to the American Revolution. This right means that the individual can express himself/herself without interference or constraint by the government. The right of free speech has been expanded to cover other means of expression that communicate a message.

Shortly after this freedom was won for the colonists, it was limited for political reasons. Congress passed the Sedition Act of 1798. *Sedition* means creating resistance to lawful authority. This law provided punishment for people found writing or speaking against the government. President John Adams and the Federalist Party used the law to retain power against the newly formed opposition party, the Democratic-Republicans. However, the law was passed with a time limit, and it was allowed to expire in 1801 while Thomas Jefferson was president.

The struggle to protect free speech and expression in the United States has been waged continually since the Bill of Rights was written. Under the First Amendment, citizens were protected from interference by the federal government. It was not until the *Gitlow v. New York* decision in 1925 that the Supreme Court ruled that the freedom of speech applied to state governments as well as the federal government. The Supreme Court has required the government to provide justification for interference when attempting to control what is being said. However, the government may prohibit some speech if it may disrupt the peace or cause violence.

Throughout the history of the United States, the greatest threats to the freedom of speech have occurred when there were threats to individuals or national security. The first laws in the twentieth century limiting speech were the Espionage Act of 1917 and the Sedition Act of 1918. These laws were designed to forbid speeches and publications that might interfere with the war effort during World War I. Since 1919 the Supreme Court has suggested that the government could limit speech representing a clear and present danger to the nation.

The interpretation of freedom of speech and expression has been expanded in the second half of the twentieth century. The Smith Act was passed in 1940, allowing prosecution for those people who were considered unAmerican in their speech and actions and who were causing a threat to the American government. In 1951 the Supreme Court upheld the Smith Act. In this case 11 leaders of the Communist Party were arrested and imprisoned for advocating the overthrow of the government.

Since the mid-1950s, the courts have seemed more concerned about the protection of personal rights and the protection of freedom of expression. The courts have recognized picketing as a form of expression and given it protection under the First Amendment. Picketing is a form of protest using actions rather than words. In 1989 the Supreme Court ruled that the government could not punish a person for burning the American flag as a form of political protest. The court found this to be a form of expression protected under the First Amendment.

Name _____

I. Reviewing the Facts
   1. The _____ of 1798 was used by the Federalist Party to restrict the work of the rival party Democratic-Republicans.
   2. Most government challenges to the freedom of speech and expression have come when there were threats to _____ or _____.
   3. Why is the burning of the American flag protected under the First Amendment?
      _____
      _____
   4. What two acts restricted speech and expression during World War I? _____ _____ and _____
   5. In 1951 the Supreme Court upheld the _____ of 1940 and allowed 11 members of the Communist Party to be imprisoned for advocating the overthrow of the government.

II. Thinking About the Story
   1. The decision to protect the rights of a person burning the American flag in protest has caused much debate across the nation. Decide whether or not you support the finding of the Supreme Court in this case. List your reasons for your decision on the lines below.
      _____
      _____
      _____
      _____
      _____

   2. Are there ever times when the government should be able to restrict the freedom of speech and expression of its citizens? Justify your answer below. Give specific reasons and examples to support your stand on this issue.
      _____
      _____
      _____
      _____

Freedom of the Press

Another important freedom guaranteed by the First Amendment is the freedom of the press. This was another of the arguments that led to the American Revolution. In 1735 John Peter Zenger, publisher of the *New York Weekly Journal*, criticized New York's Royal Governor William Cosby. A royal governor was one who had been appointed governor of the colony by the king of England. At that time criticizing the government was considered seditious libel and could be punished by death. *Seditious libel* means that untruths were published that would cause people to oppose the present government. During the trial, Zenger's attorney, Alexander Hamilton, argued that what was printed could not be called seditious libel because it was the truth. The jury freed Zenger.

Because of the case mentioned above and others that occurred throughout the colonies, James Madison included freedom of the press in the First Amendment. Its intent was to ensure that citizens had the right to report on government behavior and current events without the fear of government censorship. This means that individual citizens have the right to publish documents and to distribute those documents without getting government approval of what is written. It is important to note that no special rights or privileges have been given to a member of the press that are not also given to every other citizen. You have the right to publish facts, ideas, and opinions without interference from the government or from private groups.

Shortly after the Bill of Rights was adopted, this freedom came under fire from the federal government. The Sedition Act of 1789 not only restricted freedom of speech but also made it illegal to publish writing against the United States, either house of Congress, or the president. John Adams used this act to jail editors who supported the positions of the rival Democratic-Republican Party. The act expired in 1801 and was not renewed. However, opposition to government policies remained illegal under several congressional statutes, presidential orders, and court decisions.

Most of the restrictions placed on the press have occurred during times of war. During World War II Congress prohibited the printing of anything that might interfere with the war effort or do damage to national security. However, in more recent years such restrictions have been limited. In the 1960s and 1970s, the American press was very vocal in its opposition to the Vietnam War. In 1971 the federal government tried to stop *The New York Times* and *The Washington Post* from publishing parts of a secret study of the war called the *Pentagon Papers*. The government claimed that the publication of these papers would endanger national security. The Supreme Court ruled against the government and allowed the publication of the papers.

During the 1960s and 1970s, judges would sometimes issue "gag orders" that would prohibit the press from publishing information about ongoing trials that might violate a defendant's right to a fair trial. Examples of this information might be confessions made by the defendants or facts revealed about their past. The members of the press argued that this was a violation of the First Amendment. In 1976 the Supreme Court ruled that "gag orders" were unconstitutional except in extraordinary circumstances.

Name _____

In most cases the American press attempts to regulate itself. Most publishers will refuse material that would lead to crime, riots, or revolution. They also attempt to avoid material that is libelous, considered obscene, or offensive to large numbers of people.

I. Reviewing the Facts
1. The trial of _____ helped to create a strong desire for the freedom of the press in the colonies prior to the American Revolution.
2. In what ways did the Sedition Act of 1798 restrict the press in the United States? _____
3. It is important to note that the members of the press are not given any rights that are not also given to _____.
4. What was a "gag order"? _____
5. The media's protection against government interference was strengthened by the 1971 Supreme Court decision concerning publication of the _____.

II. Thinking About the Story
1. If you were going to set up a school newspaper, what rights and responsibilities would you have to consider? Remember, for every right that you have there is also a responsibility. Also consider that the press in the United States tries to regulate itself to avoid major problems. Explain on the lines below the rights you have and the responsibilities that you would have to consider.

_____
_____
_____
_____

2. Think about the court ruling on the "gag orders" being imposed by some judges. In your opinion, what would constitute an extraordinary circumstance that would make the "gag orders" legal in a case? Explain your answer.

_____
_____
_____

© Instructional Fair • TS Denison
IF2591 The Bill of Rights in Today's World

The Right of Assembly and Petition

The final rights granted by the First Amendment are the rights of assembly and petition. The right of assembly means that people have the right to gather for any peaceful and lawful purpose. This also implies the right to associate with groups and to share the same beliefs as the members of the group. The right to petition means that citizens of the United States have the right to ask the government for relief for any wrong they have suffered because of court or government action.

Both of these rights were important to the colonists in their struggle for independence from Great Britain. The government had attempted to outlaw meetings in which grievances against the Crown were being discussed. In some cases troops were brought out to break up the meetings. With these actions fresh in the minds of the citizens, these rights were written into the First Amendment.

The right to assemble and associate with assembled groups generally means that the government cannot require a group to register or disclose its membership. It also means that government benefits cannot be denied a person based solely on that individual's membership in a group either past or present. However, there have been a few cases in which the Supreme Court has found that government interests in disclosure and registration outweigh the interference with First Amendment rights.

The right to assemble works with the right of petition to allow people to join together to seek change from and within the government. These two rights affirm the rights of the people to participate in public life by acting in groups and by holding the government responsible for its actions. These rights are part of the bedrock of political liberty. According to decisions made by the courts, actions now covered in these freedoms include boycotts, protests, marches and demonstrations, lobbying, freedom of association, and the access to information.

Supreme Court decisions in the twentieth century have affirmed the exercise of these rights ranging from issues of civil rights to electoral politics. In 1940 the Supreme Court held that the rights of petition and peaceful assembly protect union picketing. In 1958 the freedom of association was first upheld in explicit terms when the courts overturned an Alabama law requiring organizations to disclose membership lists. In 1967 a state law requiring schoolteachers to take a loyalty oath swearing that they were not members of the Communist Party or some other organization considered subversive was overturned. In 1982 the courts ruled that a voluntary association could be used to further economic interests. This ruling stated that neither the NAACP nor its members could be held responsible for damages resulting from a legal civil rights boycott of merchants.

In general, the government is prohibited from obstructing a peaceful assembly or lawful protest based on the content being discussed. The government may, however, make reasonable regulations regarding time, place, and manner of assemblies and demonstrations as long as they are not used to deny the group's freedom entirely.

Name _____

I. Reviewing the Facts
   1. The right of _____ means that the people have the right to gather for any peaceful or lawful purposes.
   2. The right of _____ means that the people may ask the government for relief from a wrong done through the courts or through the government.
   3. What are the reasonable regulations that the government may place on a peaceful assembly or lawful protest? _____
   _____
   _____
   _____

   4. According to the courts, what actions do the rights of petition and peaceable assembly now safeguard? _____
   _____
   _____
   _____

   5. How was the right of voluntary association expanded by the Supreme Court decision in 1982? _____
   _____
   _____

II. Thinking About the Story
   1. Think about the history of the civil rights movement in the United States. How have the freedoms of assembly and petition been beneficial to this movement?
   _____
   _____
   _____
   _____
   _____
   _____

   2. In what ways do the rights of assembly and petition help safeguard the electoral political system in the United States? Among other things consider the role played by the political parties in the process. Explain how the right to assemble and petition helps to make our government the democracy it is today.
   _____
   _____
   _____
   _____
   _____
   _____

The Second Amendment
The Right of the People to Keep and Bear Arms

A well-regulated militia, being necessary to the security of a free state, the right of the people to keep and bear arms, shall not be infringed.

The story of the Second Amendment is a story straight from the American Revolution. Prior to the war, citizens in all 13 colonies were suffering to some extent from the British rules that were being enforced. Nowhere was this felt more greatly than in Boston, Massachusetts. On April 19, 1775, General Sir Thomas Gage sent British troops to Lexington and Concord to disarm rebellious patriots. To his dismay his troops met resistance, and the confrontation resulted in what is now called the "shot heard around the world."

When the British troops returned to Boston, Gage realized that a force of armed patriots had followed them and were waiting outside the city. The general told the city selectmen that a large body of men in arms had gathered and that the inhabitants of the city could be hurt if the soldiers attacked. Gage promised that the inhabitants of the city would be allowed to leave if they would turn in their weapons to a central location where they would be kept until all hostilities were ended. The citizens would then be allowed to leave the city in peace.

The city agreed to the terms offered by Gage. One could say that they actually had little choice since there was little food left in the city. British troops bullied people on the streets and were lodged in their homes, and most people were desperate to leave the city. On April 27, 1775, the inhabitants turned in 1,778 firearms. General Gage put a guard on the weapons and then announced that no one would leave the city. Word of this double cross spread quickly among the colonies.

On July 6, 1775, the Continental Congress adopted the Declaration of Causes and Necessity of Taking Up Arms that had been written by Thomas Jefferson and John Hancock. This was a strong statement condemning Gage for his actions. The following year many of the newly independent colonies began to pass bills to protect their citizens from such injustice. For example, the North Carolina Declaration of Rights adopted in 1776 stated that the people had a right to bear arms for the defense of the state. This was a way of not only claiming the individual rights of personal defense but also of proclaiming the right to overthrow the British government. Similar documents appeared in many colonies.

By the time the Constitution was written, there was a very strong feeling that the right to bear arms was necessary to protect citizens from abuses of a powerful ruling government. James Madison stated that the only protection against a strong federal army would be an armed citizenry that could fight to protect its freedom. On June 8, 1789, he proposed the list of

Name _____

rights that included the following provision: "The right of the people to keep and bear arms shall not be infringed; a well armed, and well regulated militia being the best security of a free country; but no person religiously scrupulous of bearing arms shall be compelled to render military service in person."

The Senate changed the wording of the text that was eventually adopted as the Second Amendment. The phrase "for the common defense" was proposed as an ending for the amendment. However, it was felt that such a phrase would not be interpreted as ensuring the individual's right to have arms for personal reasons as well as for the protection of the common defense.

I. Reviewing the Facts
1. General _____ sent troops to Lexington and Concord to disarm bands of rebellious colonists in those towns.
2. To be allowed to leave their city prior to the start of fighting, the citizens of Boston had to _____
3. James Madison believed that the only way to defend against a strong federal army was to have an _____.
4. Why did Congress choose not to add the words "for the common defense" at the end of the Second Amendment? _____.
5. The story of the Second Amendment is considered a major cause of the war now called _____.

II. Thinking About the Story
1. Put yourself in the place of General Sir Thomas Gage, commander of the British troops in Boston. Your troops have been fired upon and you now find a large number of armed rebels outside the city. You want to protect your men and put down this growing rebellion against your country. What actions would you have taken in this situation? Was General Gage justified in doing what he did? Explain your answers.

_____
_____
_____
_____
_____
_____
_____

2. Based on this story, what do you think was the original intent of the Second Amendment when it was added to the Constitution? Explain your answer.

_____
_____
_____
_____

© Instructional Fair • TS Denison   IF2591 The Bill of Rights in Today's World

The Second Amendment Today

The Second Amendment today is surrounded by controversy. This controversy is centered mainly on the two words *militia* and *people*. The group that supports gun control does not want the word *people* to have any meaning in the amendment. The gun rights group would not like the word *militia* to mean anything. The interpretation of this amendment takes on a different meaning when these two groups define those two words.

The best way to look at the true meaning of this amendment is to look at what the courts have said about it. Generally, the Constitution is considered to be a living document, which means that the interpretation changes to meet the needs of the times. The judges and courts of each generation provide the interpretation of the document.

The courts have consistently determined that the Second Amendment does not ensure each individual the right to bear arms. Instead, the amendment provides the right for the states to arm a militia such as the National Guard. The courts have never found a law regulating the private ownership of weapons unconstitutional. The courts have also said that the Second Amendment is not incorporated against the states. This means that the rights of this amendment are not extended to the individual citizens of the states. So a person has no right to complain about a Second Amendment violation by state laws. According to the courts, the Second Amendment only provides the right of a state to keep an armed National Guard.

I. Reviewing the Facts

1. The disagreement over the meaning of the Second Amendment centers on the two words _____ and _____.
2. The Constitution is considered to be a living document which means that _____
   _____
3. The amendment provides the right of the states to arm a militia such as the
   _____.
4. The courts have ruled that the Second Amendment is not _____ against the states, which means that the rights of this amendment are not extended to the citizens of the state.

II. Thinking About the Story
This amendment is the center of a disagreement between gun control groups and gun rights groups. Should individuals in the United States have their right to own guns protected by the Constitution? Write a brief paper explaining your views in this argument.

The Third Amendment
The Quartering of Troops

No soldier shall, in time of peace be quartered in any house, without the consent of the Owner, nor in time of war, but in a manner prescribed by law.

The story of the Third Amendment is directly related to the abuses the colonists suffered at the hands of British soldiers prior to and during the American Revolution. However, this problem of forced quartering of troops in private houses goes even further back into history. Soldiers were stationed in private homes as early as King Phillip's War (1675-1676) in both Massachusetts and Connecticut. Similar problems arose in the colonies of New York, Virginia, South Carolina, and even in Nova Scotia (Canada).

Colonial governments tried to legislate legal protection against the quartering of troops in private homes. In 1683 New York's Charter of Libertyes and Priviledges stated that no freemen would be required to house soldiers or sailors in their homes except during a time of war. This was the first time that the restriction of quartering only in the time of peace was published. However, the idea stuck and is reflected in the Third Amendment.

In 1765 Great Britain passed the Quartering Act as a means of shifting the responsibility for the financial burden caused by protecting the western frontier of the colonies from possible Indian attack. This act stated that colonists were required to bear the cost of providing barracks and supplies for British troops stationed in the colonies. The act also stated that, if barracks were not found in sufficient numbers, troops would be stationed in inns, livery stables, and ale houses. If these were not sufficient, troops would be placed in private buildings, including homes.

The problem of quartering British troops continued to be a strong issue in the colonies. After the Boston Tea Party, a new Quartering Act was passed by the British Parliament in 1774. This act authorized the quartering of troops in private homes. This act was so offensive to the colonists that it was included as one of the acts known as the Intolerable Acts.

The Declaration of Independence lists the quartering of a large number of troops among the colonies as one of the grievances against the king of England. People opposed to the war for independence warned that the Americans would also quarter troops in private houses. However, American military leaders seemed to be opposed to housing troops in private buildings. They usually built barracks, used public buildings, and tried to avoid towns.

By the end of the American Revolution, the legislatures of Delaware, Maryland, and Massachusetts had issued declarations of rights protecting their citizens from uncontrolled quartering of troops. Delaware took the lead in this issue with a provision stating that no troops could be stationed in a house without the owner's consent during peacetimes and during war only in a manner as directed by the legislature. The American dual standard that first appeared in New York's 1683 Charter of Libertyes and Priviledges was again applied in these states.

Name _____

When Madison proposed the Third Amendment to the Constitution, he stated the amendment as follows: "No soldiers shall in time of peace be quartered in any house without the consent of the owner; nor at any time, but in a manner warranted by law." Madison's amendment would have given Congress the authority to direct the quartering of troops during a time of war. However, the select committee looking at the amendments rejected this version for the one finally adopted. There has been much discussion as to why the committee rejected Madison's version. One theory is that the committee felt that the president rather than Congress should be the one directing the quartering of troops in homes in the time of war.

I. Reviewing the Facts
1. The problem of soldiers being stationed in private homes in the United States goes all the way back to _____ (1675–1676) in Massachusetts and Connecticut.
2. In 1683 New York's _____ was the first time that a restriction on quartering of troops only in a time of peace was published.
3. The New Quartering Act following the Boston Tea Party was one of the acts the colonists called the _____.
4. The _____ lists the quartering of a large number of troops among the colonies as one of the grievances against the king of England.
5. By the end of the American Revolution, the three states of _____, _____, and _____ had passed declarations against the quartering of troops in private homes during peacetime.

II. Thinking About the Story
Compare the final version of the Third Amendment with the version submitted by James Madison. What is the major difference? Why was this change made to the amendment?

_____
_____
_____
_____

Name _____

The Third Amendment Today

The Third Amendment is basically the forgotten amendment. However, it would not be true to say that it has not been violated in the history of the United States. There have been some examples in which United States troops were quartered contrary to this amendment. The most noticeable violations occurred during the War of 1812 and the Civil War.

Most of the problems with violations have come from the failure of Congress to make any laws regulating procedures for quartering troops in homes. The War of 1812 was an officially declared war with Great Britain, and troops were quartered in American homes, but Congress failed to lay down laws regulating this quartering of troops.

The Civil War raised the same issue of quartering of troops in private homes. Union troops were quartered in homes in the Southern states. When this issue was brought before the Supreme Court, the court ruled that, since the Southern states were at war with the United States, their rights under the Constitution were suspended. However, Union troops were also quartered in homes in the loyal states. In fact, this happened so many times that the military had to set up a special system to review the claims of home owners wanting rent because their homes had been occupied during the war.

The question as to how the Third Amendment was violated during the Civil War is still debated. Since Congress never officially declared war against the Confederate States, the nation was technically at peace. If this is the case, then the first part of the amendment was violated. If, on the other hand, as the Committee on War Claims insisted, the insurrection was a state of war, the second part of the amendment was violated because again Congress took no action to authorize or regulate the quartering of troops.

There has been only one major court case centered on the Third Amendment. That case was *Engblom v. Carey* in 1979. The state of New York has dorm-style residences for correctional officers on the grounds of the Mid-Orange Correctional Facility. State documents verify that this is a normal landlord-tenant relationship with those officers living here. On April 18, 1979, the correctional officers joined a statewide strike. Governor Carey sent the National Guard to the facility and housed them in the officer's rooms. The officers were locked out during the strike. The officers filed suit in court, claiming that when they returned to their rooms they found them ransacked and their personal property damaged or missing. The district court found in favor of the state, but the court of appeals reversed the decision.

Three important issues came out of the case. First, both the trial court and the court of appeals agreed that the National Guard qualified as "soldiers" under the Third Amendment. Second, this amendment was extended to the states by incorporating it into the Fourteenth Amendment. This means that the states have to guarantee this same right to their citizens. Finally, this case recognized a fundamental right to privacy in one's home. This right was applied to leaseholders as well as owners.

One issue still being debated today is whether or not homeowners have the right to compensation if troops are quartered in their homes. The Third Amendment is silent on this issue. One group argues that the Fifth Amendment gives the people the right to just compensation if their private property is seized for public use. They maintain that this right should clear the way for property owners to be compensated when troops are quartered in their homes. They argue that a constitutional right to legal constraints on quartering of troops during wartime should not be taken to deny the homeowner's rights to compensation.

The other group argues that quartering is a special type of taking. They argue that the amendment would require that homeowners consent to quartering-type takings in times of peace. During times of war, the Third Amendment would allow Congress to quarter troops and deny compensation to homeowners. According to this argument, the founding fathers felt that quartering at the expense of the homeowner would save money to be spent on other necessities to defend the country.

While some people continue to debate this issue, the Third Amendment is most often simply ignored. However, if war were to break out again in the United States, these issues would move to the surface and require consideration.

I. Reviewing the Facts
1. Most of the violations of the Third Amendment occurred during the _____ and the _____.
2. The major case dealing with the Third Amendment is _____.
3. Three important issues came out of the *Engblom v. Carey* case. What are these three issues? _____
_____
_____
4. One major issue surrounding the Third Amendment is the fact that _____ has never passed laws regulating the quartering of troops.
5. The *Engblom v. Carey* case arose from a strike on April 18, _____.

II. Thinking About the Story
There is still a debate over whether or not homeowners should be compensated if troops are quartered in their homes. Read the arguments again in the story above. Then decide whether you think homeowners should be compensated or not. Explain your reasoning below.

_____
_____

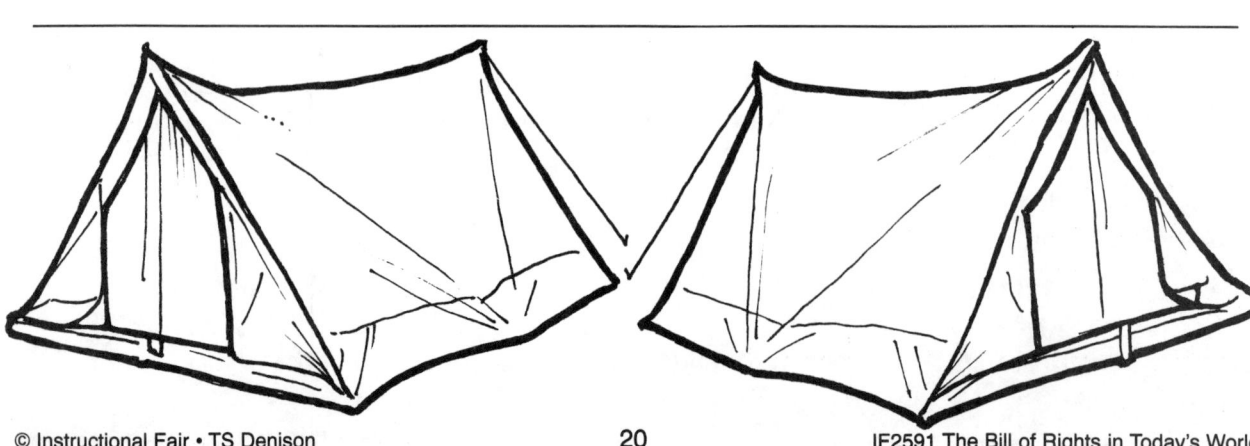

The Fourth Amendment
Freedom from Unreasonable Searches and Seizures

The right of the people to be secure in their persons, houses, papers, and effects, against unreasonable searches and seizures, shall not be violated, and no Warrants shall issue, but upon probable cause, supported by Oath or affirmation, and particularly describing the place to be searched, and the person or things to be seized.

The Fourth Amendment has been described as 54 words that are both brief and ambiguous. What the writer meant was that the amendment describes a right of the people, but it does not explain how to determine if that right has been violated. The determination of whether or not it has been violated is left up to the courts. In each case the court must decide what is a reasonable or unreasonable search or seizure.

The Fourth Amendment consists of two clauses. The first clause protects the rights of American citizens to be safe from unreasonable searches and seizures. This protection extends to your home and everything that you own. The second clause provides certain conditions that allow the issuing of a warrant authorizing a search of your property. This clause tries to set a standard as to what would be a reasonable search and seizure. The problem faced by the courts is that there is no provision for the enforcement of this right in the amendment or in the Constitution.

It is suggested that when Madison wrote this amendment he was building on the common law tradition brought over from England by the colonists. Common law is a body of law that is based on the customs of the community and on previous rulings by the courts. In England judges often ruled on cases according to the way they interpreted the beliefs of the community. Once a judge had made a ruling, other judges would base their decisions on that ruling. Eventually, the people and the courts would accept the rulings as common law.

This amendment may have been based on a controversy about the use of a general warrant by the government to conduct searches and gather evidence against citizens. Such a case arose in England between the years 1763 and 1765. John Wilkes was arrested for seditious libel. Seditious libel means that Wilkes had written papers that opposed King George III. The search and seizure of his books and papers as well as the arrest of 48 other Englishmen helped authorities gather evidence against Wilkes. This event was carried out with the use of a general warrant, allowing authorities to make any arrests or searches necessary to prove the case against Wilkes.

Knowledge of this case spread quickly throughout the colonies. At the same time, an effort was made to block the king from giving writs of assistance to customs officers in the colonies. These writs were general search warrants that allowed customs officials to enter private residences or businesses to search for goods imported illegally. The writs did not specify the place that was to be searched and were good for an unlimited period of time. English customs officials were authorized in 1762 to begin using the writs.

One year earlier, James Otis of Boston had tried to convince the Superior Court of Massachusetts that the writs of assistance were a violation of the fundamental principles of law. He was unsuccessful in his attempt. However, his efforts and the case of John Wilkes in England may have been the basis for the Fourth Amendment.

Name _____

I. Reviewing the Facts
   1. Laws that are based on the beliefs of the community and the decisions of other judges are called _____.
   2. The first clause of the Fourth Amendment guarantees the American people the right to _____.
   3. The second clause attempts to set a standard that helps determine what is a _____.
   4. The arrest of _____ in England helped to raise concern over the issuance of general warrants.
   5. _____ tried to convince the Superior Court of Massachusetts that the writs of assistance were a violation of the fundamental principles of the law.

II. Thinking About the Story
   1. The Fourth Amendment was written to prohibit the use of general warrants in the United States. Based on the story above, explain what a general warrant allowed authorities to do. Then explain how the Fourth Amendment prohibits this in the United States.

   _____
   _____
   _____
   _____
   _____
   _____

   2. If you had been James Otis trying to convince the Superior Court of Massachusetts that the writs of assistance were a violation of the principles of law, what arguments would you have used? Explain your reasoning.

   _____
   _____
   _____
   _____
   _____
   _____

The Fourth Amendment Today

What does the Fourth Amendment mean today? That seems like a simple question, but it is very difficult to answer. The main reason is that deciding what is an unreasonable search and seizure is left up to the courts. The judges trying to define these terms have had to rely on the information available to them at the time of the trial. Since our society is constantly changing, the definitions used in the cases have changed. For example, few people in the 1800s could have imagined the technology that is now available such as phones, computers, or photography. These tools have opened new ways of conducting a search and gathering evidence.

If there is a trend in interpreting the Fourth Amendment, it seems to be that the amendment protects a person's privacy. The courts had said that the citizens of the United States have a right to privacy as long as it does not disrupt the privacy of others. This belief was stated in *Boyd v. the United States* in 1886. Federal customs officials were requiring businessmen who were importing goods to show invoices or record books during the inspection of the goods coming into the country. If they did not have those documents available, the officials took the goods. The court said that these searches and seizures were a violation of the Fourth Amendment. The court further said that the protection provided by the amendment was not limited simply to entering a person's home and conducting a search. The Fourth Amendment guaranteed the individual his/her personal security, liberty, and private property, unless he/she had been convicted of a crime and given up those rights.

This court ruling gave a much broader definition of the terms *searches* and *seizures*. This definition was generally followed until the development of technology in the late nineteenth and early twentieth century brought about changes in the ways searches could be conducted. The invention of the telephone, the microphone, and the camera, among other things, brought new methods of conducting searches and gathering evidence. The question now facing the court was whether or not these were ways of conducting reasonable searches.

In 1928 the case of *Olmstead v. the United States* brought the issue of wiretapping before the court. The Federal Bureau of Investigation (FBI) had used wiretapping to collect evidence in this case. The courts ruled that wiretapping was not a method of search and seizure as recognized by the Fourth Amendment, so the FBI was following constitutional procedures. This ruling lasted for nearly 40 years.

Then in 1967 the court seemed to reverse this decision in the case of *Katz v. the United States*. Katz had been convicted of illegal gambling, based on evidence collected by a wiretap placed in a public telephone booth. The wiretap recorded conversations between Katz and his associates. The Supreme Court said that wiretapping had violated the privacy that Katz had a right to expect when using a public telephone. This violation of privacy made it a search and seizure as defined by the Fourth Amendment. The court further defined a *search* as "a government intrusion into anything in which a person has an expectation of privacy" and a *seizure* as "taking into possession or control." Not only did this case demonstrate how the interpretation of the amendment has changed, but it also strengthened the argument that the Fourth Amendment protects an individual's right to privacy.

Name _____

As early as 1914 the courts ruled that any evidence gathered in an illegal manner, without probable cause or a search warrant, would not be allowed in federal court proceedings. This ruling was designed to prevent the abuse of the Fourth Amendment by police and other government officials. If the officials knew the evidence would not be accepted in a court of law unless they followed the procedures outlined by the amendment, they would probably take more care in making certain that no searches or seizures were done without probable cause and a warrant. In 1961 the Supreme Court extended these same rules to all trials—state and federal. The court ruled that these rights belonged to American citizens at every level of government.

I. Reviewing the Facts
   1. One current trend in interpreting the Fourth Amendment is the belief that the amendment protects an individual's right to _____.
   2. In 1886 the case of _____ said that the protection of the Fourth Amendment was not limited to entering a person's home and conducting a search.
   3. In 1928 the case of *Olmstead v. the United States* found that _____ was not a method of search and seizure covered by the Fourteenth Amendment, but this decision was overturned in 1967.
   4. As early as 1914 the courts ruled that any evidence gathered without _____ _____ or a _____ _____ would not be allowed in federal courts.
   5. In 1961 these same rules were extended to all courts, both _____ and _____.

II. Thinking About the Story
   1. The Supreme Court considered the issue of wiretapping in 1928 and again in 1967. The court first declared that wiretapping was not covered by the Fourth Amendment but later reversed itself and said that it was an invasion of privacy when used in a public telephone booth. Which of the rulings do you favor? Explain your answer.

   _____
   _____
   _____
   _____

   2. How important is the right of an individual's right to privacy? Write your thoughts and then discuss this issue in class.

   _____
   _____
   _____
   _____

The Fifth Amendment
Rights in Criminal Cases

No person shall be held to answer for a capital, or otherwise infamous crime, unless on a presentment or indictment of a Grand Jury, except in cases arising in the land or naval forces, or in the Militia, when in actual service in time of War or public danger; nor shall any person be subject for the same offense to be twice put in jeopardy of life or limb; nor shall be compelled in any criminal case to be a witness against himself, nor be deprived of life, liberty, or property, without due process of law; nor shall private property be taken for public use, without just compensation.

The Fifth Amendment lists several important rights for the citizens of the United States. First, it states that no person can be tried for a capital crime or other infamous crime except by indictment of a grand jury. A capital crime is one that is punishable by death. An infamous crime is one that is punishable by either death or imprisonment. In either case, no person stands trial for a federal crime without an indictment by a grand jury. The exceptions to this law are cases during the time of war or cases in the military.

One of the early criticisms of the Constitution of the United States was that there was no guarantee of a trial by jury in civil cases. The Bill of Rights sought to correct that by making a jury trial part of three amendments. The Fifth Amendment protects the role of the grand jury. The need for such guarantees is traced back to the story of the colonists under British rule prior to the American Revolution.

Colonial grand juries had played a major role in resisting unpopular prosecutions prior to the war. In the 1730s two juries refused to indict publisher John Peter Zenger. Zenger had been charged with seditious libel for printing articles, including one that attacked New York Governor Cosby of engaging in personal attempts to avoid jury trials in civil cases. When the trial of Zenger proceeded without the indictment of the grand jury, the petite court found him not guilty. In the 1760s and 1770s, other grand juries refused to bring leaders of the Stamp Act protests and other patriot publishers and speakers to trial.

Another important part of the amendment is found in the words "due process of law." This concept of having to follow the due process of the law before depriving a person of life, liberty, or property is also stated in the Fourteenth Amendment, placing the same restrictions on the power of the states. The idea was that a person's right to life, liberty, and property was not subject to uncontrolled government power. The concept is traced back to a document called the Magna Carta that King John of England was forced to sign in 1215. The document restricted the powers of the king by stating that he could not imprison or harm a person except by a trial by peers or by the law of the land.

The amendment also states that the same government cannot try a person for a crime twice. This is referred to as the right of no double jeopardy. In other words, if a person is tried and found innocent in one federal court, that person cannot be tried for the same crime in another federal court.

The Fifth Amendment also gives citizens two additional rights. The first states that a person cannot be required to testify against himself/herself. During a trial if you hear an accused person refusing to answer a question because the answer might help to find him/her guilty, this person does so based on this amendment.

Finally, tacked on to the rights dealing with trials, the Fifth Amendment states that private property cannot be taken from a person for public use without the government paying for the property. The right of the government to take land is called *eminent domain*. This refers to taking property for public use such as for schools or building roads. This amendment states that the government must pay the owner for any property taken for public use.

I. Reviewing the Facts
  1. Under the Fifth Amendment, no person can be tried for a capital crime in a federal court without an indictment by a _____.
  2. An infamous crime is one that _____.
  3. Colonial grand juries refused to indict publisher _____, when he was accused of seditious libel.
  4. The concept of the "due process of law" can be dated back to a document called the _____ signed by King John in 1215.
  5. No double jeopardy means that _____.

II. Thinking About the Story
  1. The Fifth Amendment guarantees American citizens several rights. Decide which of these rights you believe is most important. Explain the right and your reason for choosing it below. _____

  2. The Magna Carta is a famous document signed in 1215 by King John of England. Research this important document and list five facts about it below.

The Grand Jury and Due Process of Law

Two parts of the Fifth Amendment require more explanation. The grand jury was established to protect the rights of citizens in federal criminal cases. This jury usually consists of 16 to 23 members who decide whether or not there is sufficient evidence against the accused to have a trial. They must reach a majority decision in favor of the trial before it can occur.

In many states there are two types of grand juries. The first type is the *charging jury*. The charging jury hears from a prosecuting attorney the evidence against the accused person. If the majority of the jury determine that there is sufficient evidence to prove the person guilty, they bring formal charges called an *indictment* against the accused. The case is then scheduled for trial.

The other type of grand jury is the *investigatory jury*. This jury has two major functions. First, they may examine expected wrongdoing by a public official to see if a trial is needed. Second, they may examine possible crimes, especially those carried out by organized crime. This jury may work with a special prosecutor who has been appointed just for that investigation. If a majority of the members agree that there is sufficient evidence for a trial, then they issue an indictment.

In some states and in the federal court system, these two types of grand juries are combined into one jury. This group serves both functions. The grand jury system has been criticized as being both too slow and too costly to be effective. Others argue that it is there to protect citizens from unjustified prosecution.

The second part of the Fifth Amendment that requires further discussion involves the use of the phrase "due process of law." This phrase is found in both the Fifth and Fourteenth Amendments. Its intent is to impose government fairness in dealing with people. These words prohibit local, state, or federal governments from taking a person's life, liberty, or property without following the due process of the law. One problem that still exists is that the Supreme Court has never clearly defined these words.

Because of the unclear meaning, the phrase has been applied in many ways throughout history. For example, in 1857 it was used to overturn the Missouri Compromise. This compromise prohibited slaves in certain territories of the United States. The courts ruled that the law unjustly prevented slave owners from taking their property, the slaves, into those territories. It has also been used to limit the content of some laws by declaring them unconstitutional because they restricted personal freedoms or business. Today this phrase is most often used to protect personal liberty.

Although the Supreme Court has never set the specific definitions for these words, safeguards have been developed that are often referred to as procedural due process. These safeguards have developed through both law and custom during the history of the United States. These procedures include

1. All laws must be administered fairly.
2. An accused person must be informed of all charges and given a fair hearing.
3. The person bringing charges against the accused cannot try the case.

Name _____

4. Criminal laws must be worded clearly to give adequate warning of actions that are prohibited.

These procedures now apply to all civil and criminal cases.

The grand jury and the due process of law are two ways that the Fifth Amendment works to protect the freedoms of American citizens. During the past 200 years, the interpretation of these two rights has changed and will probably continue to change in the future. However, these rights have continued to help guard people against possible government abuse of individual liberty.

I. Reviewing the Facts
1. The major task of a grand jury is to decide _____ _____.
2. The two types of grand juries are _____ and _____.
3. Sometimes a grand jury works with a _____ who has been appointed just to work with a special investigation.
4. The words "due process of law" are interpreted in various ways because the _____ has never clearly defined what they mean.
5. Safeguards that have developed to protect the "due process of law" are sometimes referred to as _____.

II. Thinking About the Story
1. There is some debate today over whether the grand jury should continue to be a part of our justice system. One group believes that it is too slow and too costly to continue, while the other side believes that it is necessary to protect the liberties of citizens. Which side of the argument do you support and why?

   _____
   _____
   _____
   _____
   _____

2. Look at the procedural due process of law that has developed through laws and customs in the United States. How do the procedures safeguard the rights of a person accused of a crime?

   _____
   _____
   _____
   _____
   _____

The Miranda Rights

The Supreme Court case of *Miranda v. Arizona* in 1966 limited the power of the police to question suspects. Ernesto A. Miranda was a warehouse worker in Phoenix, Arizona. He was arrested and charged with kidnapping and rape. During questioning by the police, he confessed, and this confession was used against him in the trial. However, he was not told of his right to remain silent and had been denied the right to consult a lawyer. The court reversed his conviction because his rights had been denied under the Fifth and Sixth Amendments.

The Fifth Amendment protects people from being forced to testify against themselves. The Sixth Amendment guarantees a defendant's right to a lawyer. The court ruled that nothing arrested persons say can be used against them in a trial unless they are told they have certain rights. Those rights include the right to remain silent and that anything they say can and will be used against them. They must also be told that they have the right to have a lawyer present during questioning and that, if they cannot afford one, the court will appoint one. If an attorney is requested, all questioning must be stopped until the attorney is present.

Since 1966 later court rulings have modified the scope of this first ruling. For example, a confession obtained in violation of the Miranda decision may now be used during a trial to prove that the defendant is lying.

I. Reviewing the Facts
1. The court decision in *Miranda v. Arizona* limited the power of the police _____ _____.
2. Miranda was a warehouse worker living in _____, Arizona.
3. The court reversed the conviction because Miranda's rights had been denied under both the _____ Amendment and the _____ Amendment.
4. A later court decision stated that a confession obtained in violation of the Miranda decision could be used in a court to prove that _____.
5. The Fifth Amendment guarantees that a person will not have to _____ _____.

II. Thinking About the Story
The Miranda Rights have been a topic of discussion since the decision was made. One group believes that these rights place too many restrictions on the police. The other side believes that they are necessary to protect the rights of the accused. What do you think about this ruling? Write a short paper (one page) stating your views and giving reasons for feeling as you do.

Name _____

The Sixth Amendment
The Right to a Fair Trial

In all criminal prosecutions, the accused shall enjoy the right to a speedy and public trial, by an impartial jury of the State and district wherein the crime shall have been committed, which district shall have been previously ascertained by law, and to be informed of the nature and cause of the accusation; to be confronted with the witnesses against him; to have compulsory process for obtaining witnesses in his favor, and to have the Assistance of Counsel for his defense.

The Sixth Amendment safeguards the right of citizens to a fair trial. The roots of this amendment go back to the experiences of the colonists in England prior to coming to the New World and during the colonial period. At times political trials were delayed in England for long periods of time. When they were held, they were sometimes held in secret. The right of the accused to a fair trial was not a major consideration during this period of history.

Some of the same problems began to arise in the colonies. Shortly after the settlers arrived at Jamestown, James Reed, the blacksmith, was condemned and hanged for refusing to follow orders. Slowly the colonists began to seek changes in the way trials were carried out. However, there was no particular consensus across the 13 colonies as to what that process should be.

The Continental Congress stated that colonists were entitled to the rights of common law. These rights included being tried by a jury of their peers according to the course of the law when accused of a crime. They further maintained that the proceedings of these trials must be made public and that the accused had the right to have witnesses and be given assistance by a lawyer. In fact, the denial of these rights to the colonies by the king of England was one of the grievances listed in the Declaration of Independence.

As already mentioned, these rights were carried out 13 different ways by the colonies, as each colony wrote its own procedures into its laws. Because of this variation, the writers of the Constitution chose not to go into specific details of criminal proceedings. However, when the Bill of Rights was added, this became one of the central rights that was included.

Under the Sixth Amendment, a person accused of a crime has the right to a prompt and public trial by an unbiased jury of his/her peers. The speedy trial would prevent innocent people from spending long periods of time in jail waiting for a trial. The jury of their peers was designed to prevent government officials from abusing their power and sentencing citizens to prison without a fair trial. The accused also must be informed of all charges. They have the right to meet face-to-face the people accusing them of the crime. The purpose of this is to prevent innocent people from being punished by testimony from unknown witnesses. The accused also have the right to face and cross-examine all witnesses that testify against them. This gives them the chance to prove whether or not the witnesses have lied or have made a mistake. Finally, the accused have the right of being defended by a lawyer. These procedures as outlined in the Sixth Amendment provide the basis for the jury trial in our legal system today.

Name _____

I. Reviewing the Facts
1. The _____ signed on July 4, 1776, listed the denial of the right of a fair trial as one of the grievances against the king of England.
2. Why were the details of criminal procedures not written into the Constitution of the United States? _____
_____
_____
3. The Continental Congress stated that colonists were entitled to the right of
_____.
4. _____, the blacksmith, was condemned and hanged in Jamestown for refusing to follow orders.
5. The Continental Congress stated that the rights of citizens included a trial by jury of their peers according to _____.

II. Thinking About the Story
Listed below are the procedures for a fair trial as given in the Sixth Amendment. Explain what each statement means and why it is important.
1. the right to a speedy and public trial _____
_____
_____
2. an impartial jury of the state and district where the crime was committed _____
_____
_____
3. to be informed of the nature and cause of the charges _____
_____
_____
4. the right to confront all witnesses against the accused face-to-face _____
_____
_____
5. the right to have witnesses to testify on behalf of the accused _____
_____
_____
6. the right to be represented by a lawyer _____
_____
_____

Name _____

The Right to a Public Trial

A criminal defendant was convicted of selling crack cocaine to an undercover police officer. However, during the trial the state trial court closed the courtroom when the undercover agent testified to protect the identity of the police officer. The case was appealed, stating that the defendant's rights to a public trial had been violated. The Appeals Court stated that the Sixth Amendment right had been violated and that the trial court should have considered alternatives to complete closure of the courtroom during the testimony. The court further ruled that the defendant must be released unless he could be retried within a reasonable time.

In 1984 the Supreme Court's decision in *Waller v. Georgia* gave four standards that must be applied to courtroom closings. Those standards are as follows:
1. The party seeking to close the hearing must have a valid reason.
2. The closure must be no broader than necessary to protect that reason.
3. The trial court must consider reasonable alternatives to closing the procedure.
4. The court must give reasons adequate to support the closing.

Discuss in a group the issues involved in this case. Then answer the following questions.

1. What was the overriding reason for closing the courtroom to the public? _____
   _____
   _____

2. What are some alternative ways that the state trial court could protect the identity of the police officer without closing the entire proceeding of the courtroom?
   _____
   _____
   _____
   _____

3. Choose the one best method of closure that you have listed above and give your reasons for supporting the closure of the courtroom in this manner.
   _____
   _____
   _____

Name _____

The Seventh Amendment
Civil Court Trials

In Suits at common law, where the value in controversy shall exceed twenty dollars, the right of trial by jury shall be preserved, and no fact tried by a jury, shall be otherwise re-examined in any Court of the United States, than according to the rules of common law.

Civil laws are laws that govern the individual rights of citizens. Thus, a civil case would be a case deciding a dispute between two citizens. The amendment uses the term common law because the writer of the amendment wanted to preserve the rights of a trial by jury in civil cases as they appeared in English common law.

This amendment again can be traced back to the circumstances surrounding the creation of the Constitution. On September 12, 1787, Hugh Williamson of North Carolina made the observation that no provision was made in the Constitution for a trial by jury in civil cases. This observation was greeted with some support, but the feeling was that the practice of handling civil cases varied so greatly from state to state that the convention would be unable to draft a suitable clause to include such a provision. However, when the Constitution was sent to the states, this became an issue that nearly caused its defeat. As a result, Madison included this amendment in his proposed list.

To understand this amendment, it is important to understand how this right was given under English common law for civil cases. The right included a trial by 12 men, in the presence of a judge who would instruct them on the law and advise them of the facts. The judge had the right to set aside their verdict if, in the judge's opinion, it was against the law or evidence. All decisions of the jury had to be unanimous. The Supreme Court has now ruled that civil juries, according to rules adopted by a federal district court, composed of six persons were permissible under the Seventh Amendment. The court felt that the framers of the Constitution were interested in preserving the right of trial by jury rather than specifying the number on the jury.

The main purpose of the amendment is to maintain the common-law distinction between the duties of the court and of the jury. The court, or the judge, determines all issues of law, and issues of fact are to be determined by the jury with instructions from the judge. This means that the jury decides whether or not the evidence proves the case. The judge determines what the law dictates as punishment.

The rights of the Seventh Amendment apply to federal courts of the United States, including courts in territories and the District of Columbia. They do not apply to state courts. However, if state courts are deciding a federally created right, the states may not eliminate the right to a trial by jury. A person does have the right to waive a trial by jury by making the request in writing.

It is interesting to note that the amendment states that any case in which an award of $20 or more is possible, the person who stands to lose the money has the right to a trial by jury. At the time of the amendment, money was based on the gold piece. The largest coin in circulation was the $20 gold piece. Today the current standard for small claims court is $400. A $20 gold piece today is worth about $400 in cash.

Name _____

I. Reviewing the Facts
  1. Civil laws are laws that _____.
  2. _____ from North Carolina made the observation on September 12, 1787, that the Constitution made no provision for a jury trial in civil cases.
  3. The main purpose of the Seventh Amendment is to _____
     _____.
  4. The rights of the Seventh Amendment apply to _____ of the United States, including courts in _____ and the _____.
  5. The original amendment states that any case in which the award exceeds _____ shall have the right to a trial by jury.

II. Thinking About the Story
  1. The rights of the Seventh Amendment were originally left out of the Constitution because the 13 states had various ways of conducting these trials. Yet the right of a jury trial in civil cases became an important issue in the debate over ratification of the Constitution. Why do you think this was such an important right in the minds of the people at that time? Do you consider it an important right today? Why?

     _____
     _____
     _____
     _____

  2. The main purpose of the Seventh Amendment is to maintain the common-law distinction between the duties of the court and of the jury. What are the duties of each of these groups?

     _____
     _____
     _____

     Why is this separation an important part of your rights as a citizen?

     _____
     _____
     _____

The Seventh Amendment Today

One of the primary purposes of the Seventh Amendment was to preserve the line separating the powers of the jury from that of the judge. At the same time the writers of the amendment sought to allow room for improving the procedures as the years passed. As a result, the court has adopted the following procedures that limit the role of a jury. Read each of these procedures and discuss how these could be helpful in a civil case. If there are any you disagree with, give your reasons for disagreeing.

1. A federal judge, during a trial, may express his/her opinion about facts, as long as all questions about the facts are ultimately submitted to the jury.

2. A federal judge may call the jury's attention to parts of the evidence that he/she believes have special importance in the case, as long as he/she distinguishes between matters of law and matters of opinion.

3. A federal judge may inform the jury when there is not sufficient evidence to justify a verdict.

4. A federal judge may require a jury to answer specific questions as well as render a general verdict.

5. A federal judge may direct the jury, after the plaintiff's case is heard, to return a verdict for the defendant on the grounds of insufficient evidence.

6. A federal judge may set aside a verdict which in his/her opinion is either illegal or goes against what the evidence proves and order a new trial.

The Eighth Amendment

Excessive bail shall not be required, nor excessive fines imposed, nor cruel and unusual punishments inflicted.

Excessive Bail

The Eighth Amendment continues to state the rights of a person accused of a crime and places limitations on the types of punishments that a convicted person may receive. The first part of the amendment states that no excessive bails shall be required of a person accused of a crime. This right was taken from the English Bill of Rights Act of 1689. The debate that has centered on this phrase is whether or not bail is to be granted to every person accused of a crime.

The Massachusetts Body of Liberties of 1641 guaranteed bail to every accused person except those charged with a capital crime or contempt in court. However, the English Bill of Rights did not provide for bail to be set in every case; it said only that bails should not be excessive where it was proper to grant bail.

Another issue was whether or not it is constitutional to withhold bail to an accused, unconvicted defendant because of the fear that the person might be a danger to the community. In 1984 Congress authorized the use of preventative detention in federal criminal proceedings. Preventative detention means that someone is held in jail without bail to protect the community.

Bail has been defined as being excessive if it is set higher than an amount that would protect the interest of the government. If the purpose of bail is to ensure that the accused will stand trial and submit to the sentence if convicted, the bail should be high enough to ensure that will happen, but no higher. If a person wishes to challenge a set bail as excessive, he/she must ask the court for a reduction. If the motion is denied, the individual must appeal to the Court of Appeals. If the motion is denied there, it goes to the Supreme Court justice presiding over that court circuit.

Excessive Fines

When the Eighth Amendment was written, the term *fine* meant a payment to a sovereign (or king) as punishment for some crime. Both the English Bill of Rights Act of 1689 and the Virginia Declaration of Rights included this phrase as a means of limiting the powers of the government. Thus the courts have ruled that the term *excessive fines* refers only to those fees imposed by and payable to the government.

Other than determining the ruling stated in the above paragraph, the courts have had little to say about the phrase. So no clear definition of what makes up an excessive fine has been given. The court has ruled that the clause does not apply to civil jury awards of damages between private parties.

Name _____

Cruel and Unusual Punishment

The last phrase of the Eighth Amendment states that cruel and unusual punishment will not be inflicted on citizens. Defining this phrase has proven to be difficult. The key question is—what is cruel and unusual punishment? There is general consensus that the writers of this amendment meant that punishments of torture, such as drawing and quartering, cutting off an ear or arm, or burning alive were considered cruel and unusual.

For guidance in determining the intent of this amendment, the courts have looked at traditional practices in the various regions, the military practice, and current writings on the death penalty. By considering these sources, the courts have upheld both death by a firing squad and electrocution as means of administering punishment. The courts even approved a second electrocution when a mechanical failure results in the injury but not death of a condemned person.

In another court case the issue was of whether or not divesting a person of his or her citizenship was cruel and unusual punishment. The court held that this punishment did qualify as cruel and unusual, because it did away with the person's status in organized society. If a person was divested of citizenship, he or she would not belong in any nation or any society. This punishment was considered equal to the methods of torture already mentioned.

Whether capital punishment (the death sentence) is a form of cruel and unusual punishment is still debated. Some groups believe that it is and should be abolished, while others maintain that it is necessary to keep order in our society. This portion of the Eighth Amendment is used as a guide for looking at the various punishments given out in our courts. Punishments are viewed in light of a basic prohibition of inhumane treatment. The laws and courts should preserve the basic concept of the dignity of man by issuing punishments within the limits of civilized society.

I. Thinking About the Story

There is still a major argument in the United States about whether or not capital punishment (the death penalty) is cruel and unusual punishment. If the courts ruled that it was cruel and unusual, then it would be unconstitutional. Think about this concept and list below arguments both for and against capital punishment. Then organize a debate within your class to determine whether or not the death penalty is unconstitutional.

Reasons for keeping capital punishment: _____
_____
_____

Reasons for abolishing capital punishment: _____
_____
_____

Name _____

I. Reviewing the Facts
   1. The first part of the Eighth Amendment states that an accused person should not be forced to pay an _____.
   2. This right was taken from the _____ written in 1689.
   3. The Massachusetts Body of Liberties of 1641 guaranteed _____ to every accused person except _____
   _____.
   4. _____ means that someone is held in jail without bail to protect the community.
   5. The term *excessive fine* has been defined by the courts as referring to _____
   _____.

II. Thinking About the Story
   1. There have been many debates over whether or not bail should be set for every person accused of a crime in federal courts. How do you feel about this issue? Are there cases in which bail should be denied? Explain your answer below.

   _____
   _____
   _____
   _____
   _____

   2. Another issue surrounding this amendment is a definition of *excessive bail*. The courts have not set a definition other than saying that it should not be higher than an amount that would protect the interest of the government. Suppose you are a member of the Supreme Court. You are to write a definition of *excessive bail* for the court. What would that definition include? Remember that you must justify everything you write by providing reasons for your decision.

   _____
   _____
   _____
   _____
   _____
   _____
   _____

The Ninth Amendment
Other Rights of the People

The enumeration in the Constitution, of certain rights, shall not be construed to deny or disparage others retained by the people.

The Ninth Amendment states that the listing of some rights in the Constitution does not deny other rights that belong to the people. One of the arguments used by the Federalists against adding a Bill of Rights to the Constitution was that if some rights were listed, someone might interpret this to mean that all other rights belonged to the government rather than the people. In the Ninth Amendment the word *enumeration* means a listing.

Madison was concerned that the Bill of Rights might be taken as an attempt to increase the power of the central government. As he addressed the Congress when presenting these amendments, he pointed out that the rights listed in the amendments as belonging to the people did not mean that all other rights belonged to the government. The Ninth Amendment was his attempt to correct any misunderstanding of the Bill of Rights. However, at the same time, it must be noted that the amendment does not specifically list any other rights of the people or any way to prevent the government from infringing on those rights.

The amendment has been interpreted to mean that there are rights of the people that exist but are not listed in the Constitution or Bill of Rights but that are protected by other provisions. The Supreme Court had not made much reference to this amendment until the *Griswold v. Connecticut* case in 1965. This case concerned a law that prohibited the use of contraceptives. The courts said that this was an infringement on the right of marital privacy. Even though the right of privacy is not addressed in the Bill of Rights, the court felt that it was guaranteed in the First, Third, Fourth, and Fifth Amendments as well as the Ninth Amendment.

The court further said that the framers of the Constitution believed that there were additional fundamental rights protected from government infringement that exist alongside those listed in the Bill of Rights. They also stated that the courts had a responsibility to interpose a veto on any attempt by the legislative or executive branch to limit or infringe on other fundamental rights. However, this ruling brings up the issue of how the courts are to determine what is fundamental and what is protected from infringement.

Name _____

I. Reviewing the Facts
1. In arguing against a Bill of Rights, the Federalists expressed fear that listing some rights might cause people to think that all other rights belonged to the _____.
2. Madison was concerned that people might see the Bill of Rights as an attempt to increase the _____.
3. The first mention of the Ninth Amendment by the Supreme Court did not occur until the case of _____.
4. The court stated that the framers of the Constitution believed that there were additional _____, protected from _____, that exist alongside those listed in the _____.
5. The ruling also brought up the issues of how the courts would determine _____.

II. Thinking About the Story
1. The Ninth Amendment does not list any specific rights or explain how to prevent the government from taking over certain rights. With this in mind, is the amendment really important? If it is important, in what ways does it make a difference in the lives of American citizens? Explain your answers below.

   _____
   _____
   _____
   _____

2. Two issues that are raised in the court decision in *Griswold v. Connecticut* are how the courts would determine which rights are fundamental and what is protected from infringement by the government. If you were a member of the Supreme Court, how would you decide whether or not a right was fundamental and protected from the government? Explain your answer below.

   _____
   _____
   _____
   _____
   _____
   _____
   _____

The Tenth Amendment
Powers to the State

The powers not delegated to the United States by the Constitution, nor prohibited by it to the States, are reserved to the States respectively, or to the people.

In order to understand the Tenth Amendment, it is important to understand the concept of federalism as defined by the founding fathers of this country. In writing the Constitution, they were trying to reach an agreement on allocation of power between the national government and that of the states. This proved to be a huge task, as each person attending the Constitutional Convention had his own ideas about how this should be accomplished. Nearly every delegate to the convention brought along a concern for the interest and security of his individual state.

The agreement that was reached in 1787 was based on compromise. At the time of the Constitutional Convention, there were two principles for organizing government. The national system was a centralized system in which the power of authority was located in one central entity. The second principle was the federal system, in which the power of the government was possessed by independent sovereign states. The Articles of Confederation provided an example of the federal system.

The Articles of Confederation had been written as the first form of government for the United States. However, problems began to arise. The power was placed in the hands of the 13 individual states. The federal government had only the powers that states allowed it to have. As a result, there was a very weak central government. The states began to act in their own best interests, which sometimes conflicted with the best interests of neighboring states. Thus, cooperation and coordination among the states were very difficult to achieve.

There was a strong feeling at the convention that the Articles of Confederation were not working and that a new system of government needed to be created. However, the supporters of the federal system mistrusted the placing of too much power in the hands of a national government. Those favoring a national system viewed a confederation as unmanageable. What both groups seemed to want was a central government that could get things done without threatening the rights and liberties of the people. Thus, the groundwork was laid for a compromise.

The question that quickly arose, however, was how to distribute powers between a national government and the state governments. This question was not answered in 1787 and continues to be a question of constitutional interpretation even today. Madison attempted to suggest a method to bring about this division. He stated that the laws of the federal government were few and defined in the Constitution. Basically the federal government would deal with external matters such as war, peace, and foreign commerce. The states, however, would have power over matters that concerned the lives of their citizens, such as life, liberty, and property and the internal order and improvement of the state.

Name _____

As the Constitution was being debated for ratification, this same question arose. Those opposing the document were concerned over the protection of the rights of the states. A strong sentiment arose for an amendment that would help to spell out this division of power. By the time the first Congress met, James Madison had an amendment in mind to address these concerns.

Madison's amendment stated, "Those powers not delegated by the constitution, nor prohibited by it to the States, are reserved to the States respectively." After debate, the words "to the United States" and "or to the people" were added. Thus, according to the Tenth Amendment, the government of the United States is a government of delegated powers. This made the United States government a new creation in models of government.

I. Reviewing the Facts
   1. The Tenth Amendment attempts to explain the division of power between the _____ and _____ governments.
   2. The two principles of organizing governments in 1787 were _____ and _____.
   3. The _____ provided the first form of government for the 13 states.
   4. What problems arose with government under the Articles of Confederation? _____
   _____
   _____
   5. As summarized in the Tenth Amendment, the government of the United States is a government of _____.

II. Thinking About the Story
   1. The division of powers between the new government under the Constitution and the states became a major issue during ratification debates. Why do you think this was such a major concern? Was this concern justified? _____
   _____
   _____
   _____

   2. If you had been a delegate to the Constitution Convention and had to choose between the national system of government and the federal system, which system would you favor? Explain your reasons. _____
   _____
   _____
   _____
   _____

Answer Key

Why Was the Bill of Rights Added?   page 2
I. Reviewing the Facts
1. May 25, 1787, at the Pennsylvania State House
2. James Madison
3. Alexander Hamilton, *The Federalist Papers*
4. Federalists and Anti-Federalists
5. New Hampshire
6. 17; 12; 10
7. George Washington
8. December 5, 1791

II. Thinking About the Story
1. Answers might include that this was the first time a government had been designed with limited powers. Up to this time all attempts to limit a government's power were done after the government had been established. This made the Constitution a unique document.
2. The Federalists would argue that there was no need for a Bill of Rights. They feared that listing some rights would be interpreted as giving all unlisted rights to the central government. The Anti-Federalists opposed a strong central government and feared that the people would lose their rights if they were not specifically listed in the Constitution.

Meet James Madison   page 4
I. Thinking About the Story
1. Answers will vary.
2. Answers might include that Madison changed his mind about the Bill of Rights because he saw that the Constitution might be defeated without these amendments. He was becoming a leader who was in touch with the wishes of the people and responded to those wishes.

The First Amendment Rights   page 5
Answers might include restrictions on religion, speech, press, assembly, and the right of petition.

Freedom of Religion   page 7
I. Reviewing the Facts
1. the establishment clause and the free exercise clause
2. Statute of Religious Liberty, 1786
3. The court said that the states had to follow the same law as the federal government under the First Amendment.
4. polygamy
5. Answers may vary but might include: Approved—bus transportation for students to church-related schools and the enforcement of the "blue laws"
Overturned—government financial aid to religious schools or reciting required prayers in the public schools

II. Thinking About the Story
1. Answers might include that with the variety of religions now being practiced across the United States, there will be a greater variety of issues to be discussed. Each religion will have its own set of beliefs and these may indeed conflict with another religion's beliefs. The issue will be how do we protect the rights of all religious groups and, at times, what makes a group a religion.

Freedom of Expression   page 9
I. Reviewing the Facts
1. Sedition Act
2. individual or national security
3. The court found the burning of the flag in protest to be a form of expression. Therefore, it is protected under the First Amendment.
4. Espionage Act of 1917 and Sedition Act of 1919
5. Smith Act

Freedom of the Press   page 11
I. Reviewing the Facts
1. John Peter Zenger
2. It became a crime to publish writings against the United States, the Congress, or the president.
3. individual citizens
4. A judge's order preventing the press from publishing information that might violate a defendant's right to a fair trial such as a confession or facts revealed about his/her past
5. *Pentagon Papers*

II. Thinking About the Story
1. Answers may vary here but might include issues such as the right to publish factual stories but the responsibility of knowing what is fact, and the right to publish the news but the responsibility of considering others' rights to privacy.

The Right of Assembly and Petition   page 13
I. Reviewing the Facts
1. assembly
2. petition
3. regulations regarding time, place, and manner of assemblies and demonstrations as long as they are not used to deny freedom entirely
4. The actions of boycotts, protests, marches and demonstrations, lobbying, freedom of association, and access to information.
5. This ruling upheld the right of a voluntary association to be used to further economic interests without being responsible for damages resulting from boycotting merchants.

The Second Amendment   page 15
I. Reviewing the Facts
1. Sir Thomas Gage
2. turn in all their weapons to a central location where they would be kept until hostilities were ended
3. armed citizenry that could fight to protect their freedom
4. It was felt that the phrase would not be interpreted as ensuring individuals the right to have arms for personal reasons.
5. the American Revolution

The Second Amendment Today   page 16
I. Reviewing the Facts
1. *militia* and *people*
2. it is interpreted to meet the needs of the time
3. National Guard
4. incorporated

The Third Amendment   page 18
I. Reviewing the Facts
1. King Phillip's War
2. Charter of Libertyes and Priviledges
3. Intolerable Acts
4. Declaration of Independence
5. Delaware, Maryland, and Massachusetts

II. Thinking About the Story
Madison gave Congress the power to direct quartering whenever the nation was at war. One suggestion for the difference is that the committee felt the executive should be able to step in during the time of war and direct the necessary quartering of troops.

The Third Amendment Today   page 20
I. Reviewing the Facts
1. War of 1812 and the Civil War
2. *Engblom v. Carey*
3. First, National Guard troops qualify as soldiers under this amendment. Second, the amendment was extended to all states. Finally, this case recognized a fundamental right to privacy in one's home and extended this right to leaseholders as well as owners.
4. Congress
5. 1979

The Fourth Amendment   page 22
I. Reviewing the Facts
1. common law

© Instructional Fair • TS Denison   IF2591 The Bill of Rights in Today's World

2. be safe from unreasonable searches and seizures
3. reasonable search and seizure
4. John Wilkes
5. James Otis

II. Thinking About the Story
1. A general warrant allowed officials to enter private residences or businesses to search without stating where the search would be made or what was being sought. There was also no time limit on the warrant. The Fourth Amendment states that a probable cause must be given supported by an oath and the place to be searched must be stated. The warrant must also state the people or things that will be seized.

The Fourth Amendment Today — page 24
I. Reviewing the Facts
1. privacy
2. *Boyd v. the United States*
3. wiretapping
4. probable cause or a search warrant
5. state and federal

The Fifth Amendment — page 26
I. Reviewing the Facts
1. grand jury
2. is punishable by either death or imprisonment
3. John Peter Zenger
4. Magna Carta
5. a person cannot be tried for the same crime by the same government a second time.

II. Thinking About the Story
1. Answers may vary but there are five important rights in the Fifth Amendment. First, a person cannot be tried for a capital crime without an indictment by a grand jury. Second, all people are guaranteed their due process under the law. Third, a person cannot be tried for the same crime twice. Fourth, a person cannot be forced to testify against himself/herself. Fifth, a person must be reimbursed for any private property taken by the government for public domain.

The Grand Jury and Due Process of Law — page 28
I. Reviewing the Facts
1. whether or not there is sufficient evidence against the accused to have a trial
2. charging jury and investigatory jury
3. special investigator
4. Supreme Court
5. procedural due process

The Miranda Rights — page 29
I. Reviewing the Facts
1. to question suspects
2. Phoenix
3. Fifth and Sixth
4. the defendant is lying
5. testify against himself/herself

The Sixth Amendment — page 31
I. Reviewing the Facts
1. Declaration of Independence
2. Each of the 13 colonies had its own procedures written into its laws for carrying out criminal procedures.
3. common law
4. James Reed
5. course of the law when accused of the crime

1. prevents innocent people from waiting long periods of time for a trial
2. prevents government officials from abusing their power and sentencing citizens to prison without a fair trial
3. makes certain accused is not being tried on charges he or she is unaware of
4. prevents innocent people from being punished by testimony from unknown witnesses
5. gives person the right to prove whether or not a witness has lied or made a mistake
6. gives the accused ability to have adequate defense

The Right to a Public Trial — page 32
The answers will vary with the exception of the first question. The overriding interest was the protection of the identity of the undercover police officer.

The Seventh Amendment — page 34
I. Reviewing the Facts
1. govern the individual rights of citizens
2. Hugh Williamson
3. maintain the common-law distinction between the duties of the court and of the jury
4. federal courts, territories, District of Columbia
5. twenty dollars

II. Thinking About the Story
1. The people had just overthrown a government that they had not trusted. One area that had been in issue was the ruling of the courts in favor of the Crown. The citizens wanted to ensure that the new government would have fair courts.
2. The judge determines all issues of law including the appropriate punishment and gives instructions to the jury. The jury decides whether or not the evidence proves the case.

The Eighth Amendment — page 37
I. Reviewing the Facts
1. excessive bail
2. English Bill of Rights Act
3. bail; those charged with a capital crime or contempt in court.
4. Preventative detention
5. fees imposed by and payable to the government

The Ninth Amendment — page 40
I. Reviewing the Facts
1. government rather than the people
2. power of the central government
3. *Griswold v. Connecticut*
4. fundamental rights, government infringement, Bill of Rights
5. what is fundamental and what is protected from infringement by the government

II. Thinking About the Story
1. Answers may include that this amendment is important because it points out that those rights listed in the amendments are not the only rights of the people. There are other rights that belong to the people and not to the government. It also has been interpreted by the Supreme Court to mean that it is their duty to declare unconstitutional any laws that would restrict or limit the fundamental rights of the people.

The Tenth Amendment — page 42
I. Reviewing the Facts
1. national government, state
2. national system and federal system
3. Articles of Confederation
4. The central government had little or no power. Since the states had the power, they began to work in their own best interests. There as little cooperation and coordination among the states.
5. delegated powers

II. Thinking About the Story
1. Answers will vary but one possible answer was that the colonies had just fought to gain freedom from a king who claimed total authority over them. They were afraid the new national government might do the same thing.